About

My purpose for writing this book is because I discovered that there are very few books on pastoring. This is especially true for first time pastors who shepherd a small church.

There are many books written on how to preach, but very few on pastoring. So after pastoring for 33 years and pastoring six different churches in those 33 years, I decided to write a book to pastors about how to pastor and grow a small country church.

During those 33 years of pastoring, I have pastored very small churches that varied in size. One which consisted of 34 members, a church with 50 members, and one might have had 75 members, another one with 125 members, and of course two with 500 members.

I discovered that there are some things that all small churches have in common whether they were located in the country or in the city. Most importantly is, that there are some things that every pastor who is pastoring a small church should know. This is what I have tried to address in this particular book.

You will be blessed if you read this book and apply the principles that I have written in this short book, mainly because I have tried these principles. These basic principles have worked at all six churches and the people were blessed. It is my hope that you and your church will be blessed through this book.

HOW TO PASTOR AND GROW A SMALL CHURCH

Reverend Carl Hughes, Pastor Emeritus
Rose Hill Missionary Baptist Church
Magnolia, Mississippi

Preface

This title of "How to Pastor a Country Church" is dedicated to all the Pastors who serve small congregations who have a servant heart with the desire to grow yourself and the membership both spiritually and financially. This is preacher to preacher, from one servant pastor to another, for all of the pastors who care about the church of whom God has given you charge with.

First, picture yourself sitting in a Pastor's study. The Senior Pastor is here, other well-known Pastors are there and you are sitting in the midst. It is at that time where you can gain from their wisdom as they converse with one another about pastoring small congregations, the good and the bad.

They talk about the great things God is doing and often times they share some things they should not have done. Some of the jewels that they share are priceless. On some occasions you will hear them say, that which I knew was the right thing to do, was not done in the right timing, because it was done in the wrong season according to the move of God.

This is my "notes from the Pastor's Study" that I would like to leave for the pastor of a small church.

Contents

I. FOUNDATIONAL TRUTH (1)

II. HOW TO INCREASE THE FINANCES IN HIS CHURCH (3)

III. HOW TO START MINISTRIES IN CHRIST'S CHURCH (11)

IV. MINISTRIES THAT I BELIEVE NEED TO BE IMPLEMENTED (17)

V. THE ADVANTAGE OF ROTATING LEADERS IN THE CHURCH (21)

VI. KEEPING THE OLDER MEMBERS AND ATTRACTING YOUNGER MEMBERS (22)

VII. START A YOUTH CHURCH MODELED ON VACATION BIBLE SCHOOL (24)

VIII. LAYMAN MINISTRY (24)

IX. FIRST TIME PASTORS (26)

X. SOLVING PROBLEMS IN THE CHURCH (28)

XI. NOT GETTING TRAP BY PROMINENT FAMILIES IN THE CHURCH (30)

XII. DON'T FORGET GOD IN YOUR GROWING AS A PASTOR (31)

XIII. THE SIN OF JUDGING OTHERS ON THEIR PREACHING ABILITY (33)

XIV. AS A PASTOR, DON'T NEGLECT THE CHURCH BUILDING OR ITS GROUNDS (35)

XV. FUNERALS (36)

XVI. HELPING THE CHURCH TO FIND HER NEXT PASTOR (39)

XVII. KNOWING WHEN TO HOLD THEM AND WHEN TO FOLD THEM (40)

XVIII.	PREPARING FOR RETIREMENT (44)
XIX.	CHURCH CONFERENCES (47)
XX.	THE PASTOR AND HIS HEALTH (48)
XXI.	THE PASTOR'S SPIRITUAL LIFE (49)
XXII.	THE PASTOR DEALING WITH TEMPTATIONS (51)

I. <u>FOUNDATIONAL TRUTH</u>

"But you, Daniel, Shut up the words, and seal the book until the time of the end, many shall run to and fro (world travel will increase dramatically) and knowledge shall increase." (Daniel 12:4 KJV)

"Study to shew thyself approved unto God, a workman that needeth not to be ashamed, rightly dividing the word of truth." (2 Timothy 2:15 KJV)

Buckminster Fuller created the "Knowledge Doubling Curve"; he noticed that until 1900 human knowledge doubled approximately every century. It is believed by the end of World War II knowledge was doubling every 25 years. Today things are not as simple as different types of knowledge have different rates of growth.

For example, knowledge about the atom is doubling every two years and clinical knowledge every 18 months. But on average human knowledge is doubling every 13 months. According to IBM, the build out of the "internet of things" will lead to the doubling of knowledge every 12 hours.

IBM's new Watson *Internet of Things* (*IoT*) is a cognitive system that learns from, and infuses intelligence into the physical world. All we have to do now is "Ask Watson".

This is of course artificial intelligence, but you oh Man of God is depending on the voice of the one who called you and the wisdom of the elders per se.

II. <u>HOW TO INCREASE THE FINANCES IN HIS CHURCH</u>

Use the offering time as a time to teach God's people about giving. Read scriptures and explain them during the offering, so the people will know what God's word say about giving. Because it takes money to operate ministries in the church.

The reason most small churches do not get involved in ministries is because of the lack of money. I believe every church is geographically located in its place for a reason. The reason is to minister to those in that area.

<u>Tithe Pledge Scriptures</u>:

These are scriptures that are commonly found in church programs given out each Sunday prior to worship service. This example is taken from a former church I pastored and I think serve in a minor role as Pastor Emeritus of the Rose Hill Missionary Baptist (RHMBC), Highway 48 East Magnolia, Mississippi where

Pastor Gary Brumfield is now serving as my Pastor.

Leviticus 27:30 (KJV) And all the tithe of the land, *whether* of the seed of the land, *or* of the fruit of the tree, *is* the LORD'S: *it is* holy unto the LORD.

Malachi 3:10-12 (KJV) [10] Bring ye all the tithes into the storehouse, that there may be meat in mine house, and prove me now herewith, saith the LORD of hosts, if I will not open you the windows of heaven, and pour you out a blessing, that *there shall* not *be room* enough *to receive it*. [11] And I will rebuke the devourer for your sakes, and he shall not destroy the fruits of your ground; neither shall your vine cast her fruit before the time in the field, saith the LORD of hosts. [12] And all nations shall call you blessed: for ye shall be a delightsome land, saith the LORD of hosts.

1 Corinthians 16:2 (KJV) Upon the first *day* of the week let every one of you lay by him in store, as *God* hath prospered him, that there be no gatherings when I come.

2 Corinthians 8:12-15 (KJV) [12] For if there be first a willing mind, *it is* accepted according to that a man hath, *and* not according to that he hath not. [13] For *I mean* not that other men be eased, and ye burdened: [14] But by an equality, *that* now at this time your abundance *may be a supply* for their want, that their abundance also may be *a supply* for your want: that there may be equality: [15] As it is written, He that *had gathered* much had nothing over; and he that *had gathered* little had no lack.

2 Corinthians 9:7-11 (KJV) [7] Every man according as he purposeth in his heart, *so let him give*; not grudgingly, or of necessity: for God loveth a cheerful giver. [8] And God *is* able to make all grace abound toward you; that ye,

always having all sufficiency in all *things*, may abound to every good work: [9] (As it is written, He hath dispersed abroad; he hath given to the poor: his righteousness remaineth for ever. [10] Now he that ministereth seed to the sower both minister bread for *your* food, and multiply your seed sown, and increase the fruits of your righteousness;) [11] Being enriched in every thing to all bountifulness, which causeth through us thanksgiving to God.

Galatians 6:9-10 (KJV) [9] And let us not be weary in well doing: for in due season we shall reap, if we faint not. [10] As we have therefore opportunity, let us do good unto all *men*, especially unto them who are of the household of faith.

    You should to the best of your ability teach your congregation to "Focus on being content with God's daily provisions". This is also included as part of church program bulletin.

Read the following verses. Think and pray about the verse that applies the most to your life.

God's Daily Provisions Scriptures

1 Timothy 6:6-8 (ESV) [6] But godliness with contentment is great gain, [7] for we brought nothing into the world, and we cannot take anything out of the world. [8] But if we have food and clothing, with these we will be content.

Ecclesiastes 5:10 (ESV) He who loves money will not be satisfied with money, nor he who loves wealth with his income; this also is vanity.

Proverbs 30:8-9 (ESV) [8] Remove far from me falsehood and lying; give me neither poverty nor riches; feed me with the food that is needful for me, [9] lest I be full and deny you and say, "Who is the LORD?" or lest I be poor and steal and profane the name of my God.

Matthew 6:9-11 (ESV) [9] Pray then like this: "Our Father in heaven, hallowed be your name. [10] Your kingdom come, your will be done, on earth as it is in heaven. [11] Give us this day our daily bread."

Philippians 4:11-13 (ESV) [11] Not that I am speaking of being in need, for I have learned in whatever situation I am to be content. [12] I know how to be brought low, and I know how to abound. In any and every circumstance, I have learned the secret of facing plenty and hunger, abundance and need. [13] I can do all things through him who strengthens me.

"You are only poor when you want more than you have. The trouble with most people is their earning capacity doesn't match their yearning capacity. The most expensive vehicle to operate, per mile, is the shopping cart". (Unknown Author)

Bottom line, use any of this material to aid your ministry and feel free to come up with your own as you are inspired by the Holy Spirit of spirit minded members of your congregation.

III. <u>HOW TO START MINISTRIES IN CHRIST'S CHURCH</u>

Remember the church doesn't belong to you. You should consider it an honor to be chosen from among other men to lead God's people. If the truth be told none of us are qualified on our own merits.

Christ's church need leaders who know that *they are saved* and know *they have been called to preach*. It is a sad thing for a church to have a pastor who has not been saved nor called to preach.

"Pastor I hope you have been saved and called".

Christ's church is in need of leaders who need the two things mentioned above. But I also believe no man is elected as pastor of Christ's church without God's perfect or permissible will, save or unsaved.

The saved sent to develop his people and the unsaved to discipline his people. I base this on Jer. 3:15 where God said I will give you shepherds/pastors according to mine own heart.

I attended a lecture hosted by Alcorn State University in the early eighties, the lecturer was Dr. Gardner C. Taylor. He said the time is upon us that we, as pastors, can no longer be content just to get God's people on a spiritual high on Sunday morning and just send them home to fend for themselves the rest of the week. The church has to be concerned about the whole man. This is where ministry comes into play. People are hurting especially the young and the old.

Jesus talked about ministries in Matthew 25:35-46 (KJV) [35] For I was an hungred, and ye gave me meat: I was thirsty, and ye gave me drink: I was a stranger, and ye took me in: [36] Naked, and ye clothed me: I was sick, and ye visited me: I was in prison, and ye came unto me. [37] Then shall the righteous answer him, saying, Lord, when saw we thee an hungred, and fed *thee*? or thirsty, and gave *thee* drink? [38] When saw we thee a stranger, and took *thee* in? or naked, and clothed *thee*? [39] Or when saw we thee sick, or in prison, and came unto thee? [40] And the King shall answer and say unto them, Verily I say unto you, Inasmuch as ye have done *it* unto one of the least of these my brethren, ye have done *it* unto me. [41] Then shall he say also unto them on the left hand, Depart from me, ye cursed, into everlasting fire, prepared for the devil and his angels: [42] For I was an hungred, and ye gave me no meat: I was thirsty, and ye gave me no drink: [43] I was a stranger, and ye took me not in:

naked, and ye clothed me not: sick, and in prison, and ye visited me not. [44] Then shall they also answer him, saying, Lord, when saw we thee an hungred, or athirst, or a stranger, or naked, or sick, or in prison, and did not minister unto thee? [45] Then shall he answer them, saying, Verily I say unto you, Inasmuch as ye did *it* not to one of the least of these, ye did *it* not to me. [46] And these shall go away into everlasting punishment: but the righteous into life eternal.

    This is where deacons are needed to help God's people. I believe deacons play a major role in carrying out the mandate in Matt. 25:35. But first I believe most deacons need to be trained as leaders in order that they will know how to help lead God's people in ministry.

    I believe the pastor should meet with the deacons on a weekly basis to train them how to be good leaders and to keep him informed of what is happening in the church and also keep himself informed.

Meet with them during Sunday school hour. After deacons have been trained and ministries have been organized. Deacons should be assigned to the ministries. Each deacon to certain ministries as a deacon advisor/leader to work with the leader of that ministry.

I also believe we should call everything we do a ministry instead of the term auxiliary and call the persons who are responsible for these ministries leaders and co-leaders. You need help in pastoring Christ's people and this is where deacons come in as assistants. Give deacons and leaders jobs description. Reasons for this is that they will know their duties as deacons and leaders. A pastor's reference material on this subject, <u>Maxwell Leadership Bible</u> by John Maxwell is the book I recommend.

We as pastors need a helping hand in shepherding God's people because Christ said the works that I do, greater works shall you do. John 14:12 (KJV) Verily, verily, I say unto you, He that believeth on me, the works that I do shall he do also; and greater *works* than these shall he do; because I go unto my Father. Jesus was concern about the whole man during his stay on earth and so should his church.

IV. <u>MINISTRIES THAT I BELIEVE NEED TO BE IMPLEMENTED</u>

Feeding the elderly in your congregation.

Seniors citizens are having a hard time when comes to food and prescriptions being filled because of the lack of money. The church should help in these areas as much as possible. As I said it takes money to do ministry. This is where food banks/meals on wheels comes into play. These should start small and then expand as resources allow.

Helping members when they lose their jobs.

Churches should have a ministry to help members find employment who want to work. Personal loans $250 for member in good standing. There are a great number of our people who are living from pay check to pay check who some time need a helping hand not a gift but a loan to make ends meet. This money is loaned interest free. I recommend these requirements for the loan. Members must be active members. They are given thirty or sixty days to repay the money.

Helping members when their homes burn.

As soon as possible, give them at least $500. Most churches wait until Sunday before they do anything for people who have lost their home. Due to fire people need help the same night of same day. This is a ministry in itself because these people need a place to stay and clothes. This is where the five hundred dollars come into play, but you should still do the offering on Sunday with gift cards.

Help seniors' citizens with utilities who need it twice a year.

This is supported by members who want to help with this ministry. The church can seed this ministry from day one. Guidelines would need to be developed to establish what senior citizens are entitled to the money.

Give scholarship for seniors finishing high school and enrolling in college.

Have you noticed that when our children are on the national stage they give thanks to everyone except there local church the reason for that is because their local church hasn't done anything to help them get where they are. If our churches would be concerned about the whole person our children would be more thankful to their local church. One way to fund the scholarships is have a special offering during the reassembling of the Sunday School. The money may not seem to be much but if it's done every week this can add up to quit a bit at the end of a year. Most small church don't have more than one or two children graduating each year. I suggest starting the scholarship program off with five hundred dollars and as the money increase give more too each student.

V. **THE ADVANTAGE OF ROTATING LEADERS IN THE CHURCH**

Leaders need to be changed in the ministries at least every four years. Reason for this is that it gives all who have a desire to lead an opportunity to lead and keep new ideals coming into the ministries. Another reason it keeps any one person from taking ownership of that ministry. Once a person take ownership of a ministry it is hard for anyone to replace them even the pastor. Weather the leader is a good leader or bad leader. What I recommend is the person be rotated as leader of that ministry every two to four years. They can serve again after two years' time period. Leaders must have a job description.

People make better followers once they have had a taste of leading people. The disadvantage of this system is that the ministry may suffer if the former leader leave the ministry. It is important that the old leader train the new leader for at least three to six months

VI. <u>KEEPING THE OLDER MEMBERS AND ATTRACTING YOUNGER MEMBERS</u>

This is one of the hardest things a pastor has to do but he must do it because the ministries of the church depend on it. A pastor must remember that he needs the older members because they are the ones who holds the strings to the purse. He needs the young members because they can fill the pews now and in the future. The problem he has with these two groups is that they don't think that they need each other. The old think the young is out to get their positions in the church. And the young think the old need to sat down and let them do everything. The pastor has to find a way to let both groups know that they need each other because they really do. One way to do this is to let both groups know that the church needs both. In order for the church to do ministry now and in the future. The older members know what need to be done but they are too old to do it and the young are young enough to do things but don't what to do but together they can do the impossible.

    Revamping the Sunday School I recommend this book: <u>Fulfillment Hour</u> compiled and edited by George O. McCalep, Jr Ph.D. Subject: <u>Fulfilling God's Purposes for the Church Through the Sunday School Hour</u>, by Jackie S. Henderson and Joan W. Johnson.

VII. **START A YOUTH CHURCH MODELED ON VACATION BIBLE SCHOOL**

Have you ever wonder why our local church can get hundreds of children out for vacation bible school and can only get thirty out for Sunday School and church on Sunday morning.

I believe it is the way the two events are designed. In vacation bible school the children are involved activities during the whole session but during Sunday school they are spectators. I believe if we would use the vacation bible school pattern we would get the same results using the same dress code also.

VIII. **LAYMAN MINISTRY**

Layman ministry helping senior citizens with things they can't do for themselves nor can they pay someone else to do them. Two examples are mowing the lawn during the summer months. Building handicapped ramps.

Whatever it takes to make life a little easier for them.

Hospitality ministry greeting peoples on Sunday morning. Wal-Mart have persons waiting to welcome the customers to their store. Our churches need to follow the lead of the corporate world in this area.

Associates ministers can be a blessing or a curse to a senior pastor. Some associated ministers will never pastor. They will be with the senior pastor their entire stay in that church.

They have no desire to pastor. If that be the case find somethings for him to do that is useful to you and the church.

If you need more help than usual as senior pastor make one associate your assistance pastor and not the church assistance pastor reason being if he is not teachable you can always replace him without the approval of the church.

IX. FIRST TIME PASTORS

It is important that a first time pastor seek the advice of an older pastor on some dos and don'ts about pastoring because there are some.

Find a mentor and pick his brain for information about pastoring in general. One general rule that I operate by is that when I am around pastors who are more experience and have more knowledge about pastoring than I have, I speak very little except to ask questions.

Reason I already know what I know but I need what they know also. You can learn from pastors good decisions as well their bad decisions. So listening is a good tool to employ when around seasoned pastors.

Before you make changes make sure you understand why it need to be changed. Make sure what you are implementing is better than what is in place. Everything that is being done in the church is not tradition. It has to do with the culture of that church and the culture of the time when it was implemented. No two churches are alike in worship and structure. A year should pass before a new pastor make any major changes.

Pray that God will give you a vision for that church because without a vision you will not be able to move the people forward. Your first year at that church should be spent seeking God's purpose for placing you at that church. So rather than making major changes spend that time seeking god face for a vision for that church.

First time pastors will make mistakes in their pastoring. Learn from your mistakes and don't make the same mistake again. Because some mistakes you can recover from and some you cannot that's why it important to seek the council of older seasoned pastors to help you as you learn how to pastor.

X. SOLVING PROBLEMS IN THE CHURCH

As a pastor you have to be a problem solver because God's people are a problematic people. If they didn't have problems they wouldn't need you. So you need to read and study books dealing with church conflicts. The better you are with intervening in the conflicts, the easier it will be in your PASTORING.

You don't need to intervene in every conflict that arises in the church because some of them will take care of themselves. When you do have to intervene, don't take sides with either party. What you want to do is get the two parties back in a working relationship. Because conflicts can get to the point of no return where it doesn't matter whose right or what's right, it's a matter of who wins and who loses. The more you do this, the better you will get as a problem solver.

Then you start looking at problems as a learning experience for you and God's people. Something new will always come out of the old. New attitudes new interactions. So don't lose you cool when problems arise, it's God's way of growing you as a pastor and growing his people.

XI. <u>NOT GETTING TRAP BY PROMINENT FAMILIES IN THE CHURCH</u>

Most first time pastors in small rural churches fall into the trap of being won over by the most prominent family in the church. With gifts and others perks, such as being invited to their homes after church on Sunday. This will lead to you feeling indebted to this family.

If you do this you will be obligated to eat at every family that gives you an invite to have dinner with them. This will only lead to confusion in the end, because the first time you refuse an invite, you now have picks in where you will eat dinner.

Every family wants bragging rights that the pastor ate dinner at our home. I believe it's best not to start eating dinner in members' home in this day and time. If families want to feed the pastor and his family implement a plan for each church family to pay for himself and his family's meal at a local restaurant.

XXII. <u>DON'T FORGET GOD IN YOUR GROWING AS A PASTOR</u>

As a pastor don't forget you are where you are because of God's arranging, appointing and assigning you to your appointment as pastor of his church, so be careful and don't get lifted up in pride and think you are all that. Whatever gifts you may have, they are God's gifts and not yours. He gave you those gifts through the Holy Spirit. He gave them and he can take them away. It's all about the mind, lose your mind and you lose the gifts.

A sound mind is what it's all about. When God wakes you up in your right mind, that's where your day begins as a pastor. Without your right mind, you are just another man among many other men, but because of your mind and your gifts, you are God's pastor after his own heart. It's very easy to forget whose you are and who you are.

You are God's pastor/preacher. You are God's gift to his church. God called and sent you and God can recall and un-send you. Just remember God can fire you and he will fire you, but only if you refuse to remember whose you are and who you are. When he fires you, nobody else can hire you. Before he fires you though, he will lay you off for a season and bring you back to work. So always remember God and his people can get along without you. They were doing pretty good before you were born and they will be doing pretty good after you gone.

XIII.   **THE SIN OF JUDGING OTHERS ON THEIR PREACHING ABILITY**

Some preacher/pastors get lifted up in pride when God blesses them with a good voice to preach with and good tools to enhance their voice in delivery of God's message. Sometimes they begin to judge those preachers who God has not blessed or favored with the voice nor the tools to study with.

If the truth be told no preacher has arrived yet in this thing called gospel preaching. All preachers should be striving to be like the prince of preachers Jesus the Christ. The best preacher in the house can learn something from the worst preacher who is preaching or who has just preached. Jealousy among pastors/preachers is the biggest problem that exist in the ministers' rank.

I believe it is one of the things ministers bring with them from the pews after they are called to preach. What we need to learn is that all preachers don't have the same potentials. It has to do with our educational background and our mastery of words in the English language. The more words you have within the faculty of your mind to command, the better picture you can paint with words for God's people. We have to accept every pastor/preacher for who he is, because every man has to give account to his own master Jesus the Christ.

    All of us are limited to what we can do for God's people. We are not sent to do it all, only what we are sent to do and whatever that is, we need to make sure we do our very best. Because to who much is given much is required.

    The late L.E. McEwen said, "God has given no man all of it, but has given every man enough to make it on, if he develops what God has given him". So be thankful for whatever God has blessed you with and if you want more, you need be like Jabez, pray to God and ask him to increase your territory which means more responsibility in your ministry.

XIV. AS A PASTOR, DON'T NEGLECT THE CHURCH BUILDING OR ITS GROUNDS

Sometimes as pastors, we become so heavenly minded until we are no earthly good. We should be so heavenly minded until we are some earthly good. You need to be concerned about the status of the church building. Make sure needed repairs are done as needed. I believe it's a reflection on the pastor when the church building is not maintained properly. The church building should be neat and clean and somebody has to make sure this is done. The church lawn should also look presentable at all times. I am not saying the pastor should do these things because if he does, when he stops no one else will start but he needs to give the responsibility to someone else and to make sure it is done on a regular basis.

XV. FUNERALS

Conducting Funerals are a part of pastoring. It is a time when you are caring for God's people. I believe it's very important for the pastor to make contact with the bereaved family as soon as possible, because that's when you are pastoring. Pastoring is more than eleven o'clock on Sunday morning. You being there means more than you can ever imagine. You may be at a loss for words, but that's alright. You are God's representative and when you are there the family feel that God is there with them. Let the family know that you are there to help them through this troubling time.

During the funeral your main goal is to help the family get past the death of their love one. Sometimes we pastors forget the bereaved family in our message and spend more time talking to other people rather than helping the immediate family members.

I discovered that the families setting on the front pews are the ones who are still hurting during the funeral and rather than helping them we turn this time into a celebration. I noticed there is very little celebrating on the front pews, but the further you get from the front pews, the more celebration takes place. I know we can't control other people actions, but please don't forget you are there to help the family and not to hurt them. They have enough hurt to last awhile, so let's not add to it.

There are some very good reference books that are a must have for pastors that will aid you with conducting a funeral service. It is highly recommended that you have one with you during these occasions especially if you are new and inexperienced. They are <u>Boyd's Pastor Manual for the Pastor, Preacher and Parish</u> and/or <u>The STAR BOOK for MINISTERS</u> by Edward T. Hiscox. By using these tools as your reference, you present yourself in a more professional way. You must also read the material regularly, so in the time of need, you will not appear to be fumbling and looking unprofessional.

XVI. **HELPING THE CHURCH TO FIND HER NEXT PASTOR**

I believe the pastor after God' own heart who loves God's people and his task has been completed at a particular church and he is obedient to God's call on his life and he knows it's time for him to move. If he really loves the people that God has allowed him to pastor he should start looking for his successor that he can start mentioning him so he will know what's going on with the people and ministries in the church. Now this will only work if you are retiring not leaving for another church. If you are leaving for another pastoral position I believe it best to help set up a search committee and inform the committee what their duties are if they will let you. I know churches have by-laws which says the pastor should give the church thirty days' notice before leaving. I have found that doesn't work with most church's because if the people still love you they will become angry with you and don't want to hear anything thing you have to say.

XVII. <u>KNOWING WHEN TO HOLD THEM AND WHEN TO FOLD THEM</u>

Kenny Rogers wrote a song with this title about a gambler in a card game. I think this is true when PASTORING people. The method of pastoring has changed in the past fifty years. There was a time when dictatorship was the norm in pastoring. When the pastor rule with an iron hand and things usually went the way he wanted them to go.

The people didn't have a lot of input in the direction that the church would travel. But times have changed and people want to share in leadership in the church. It's what I call participated leadership. They want to have a real voice in the decisions that are made in direction the church will travel.

There was a time when people didn't question the authority of the pastor in him making decisions about leading the church. But now every decision the he make is in question and he has to have an answer that makes sense to the people and be willing to make adjustments to his decision as needed. He may only get some of the things he wanted but something is better than nothing.

    There was a time when a pastor could pastor a church for forty or fifty years. That day is gone, also that's not the norms anymore. I think it is more like ten to twenty or thirty years. I believe the pastor knows before the people know when his time has ended as pastor. Because when his time has ended he no longer can lead the people forward and they become stagnant and refused to move FOWARD under his leadership.

    Every God sent pastor has a purpose for being at that particular church and when that purpose has been completed its time to go. And sometimes the purpose has not been completed and it is still time to depart. I believe God gives a church a pastor after his own heart for one or two reasons to develop them or to discipline them either way both has a beginning and ending and a pastor has to know when he has completed his purpose.

Please Note: There also seem to be the case of when the local church are so bad in the eyes of God, that He will send them pastors after their heart.

Because once a pastor has completed his task, he is no longer supposed to be there. He is supposed to be somewhere else and someone else is suppose be where he is. I believe God moves his pastors around as a chess player moves his players on a chess board. We belong to God and he does exactly as he pleases with his own. God will take care of his pastor if he is obedience to his voice in staying and moving with his church. Ok now sometimes as a pastor, we think a church cannot make it without you but it can.

Sometimes it will do better without you when your purpose has been completed.

Illustration: It is like a woman who has a husband and she is doing everything she can to show him that she loves him and he leaves her for another woman. She is hurt and becomes very, very angry, but if she doesn't love him, and all her actions say she doesn't, then she is glad he is leaving so she can find someone else.

The Sunday you tell the church that you are leaving for another church do it after you preach and before you dismiss, because it will be like a funeral when you tell the church that you are leaving that is if they love you. If they don't love you, it will be like a family reunion.

XVIII. <u>PREPARING FOR RETIREMENT</u>

When the senior pastor began to advance in age, he should start looking for his successor and start mentoring him at least four years before his retirement. I believe a pastor with a pastor's heart will love the church enough to accept the fact he is no longer able to lead God's people to a higher level and his pastor's heart will help him make this difficult decision because of his love for the people. This is why he needs to start preparing for his retirement when he is young.

Get the church to start a retirement account that they will pay into on a monthly basic. Start saving some of your pastor's appreciation money. Start getting yourself debt free by the age of sixty five and use the next five years to save as much as possible. Get the church to continue to pay into your retirement for at least ten years after you retire. Start your successor retirement with less than what you are getting because he will have years to build his account.

But the reality is most young pastors don't believe they are going to get old. They do not consider a time where they won't be able to preach or teach and pastor like they use too. But everyone in this world gets old if they don't die young, and age brings a lot of inconveniences with it. It is better to retire on your own terms than on the church.

It is better for them to be crying than you. God is able to sustain us after we retire. It's a matter of faith and believing God will take care of his own. Give young ministers an opportunity to preach while you are pastoring because most of them will become pastors in the coming years and as the sun is setting on you, it will be rising on them. They won't forget how you befriended them in the early years of their ministry. They will let you preach when you are old because you let them preach when they were young, and God's people won't miss a beat in moving forward in kingdom building.

XIX. CHURCH CONFERENCES

Church conference every month is becoming a thing of the past in larger Churches, but for smaller church conferences are still alive and well.

If we're you pastoring a church that still have conference on a regular basis, this is what I suggest. Don't have conference any place other than the sanctuary. Reason being the conference will be in the same place that the people worship God on Sunday. The pastor should never come down onto the level of the people by sitting where the deacons sit. The pulpit is the only place of authority.

You can moderate the conference better from the pulpit. You should always remain standing during the meeting. You should never sit and yield the floor to someone else as long as you are standing. People can only speak by you acknowledging them to speak. When you sit and someone else stand, you are faced with task of getting the floor back from them.

Always have a printed agenda. No business will be discussed in the particular conference, if it is not on the agenda. Reason being you and your leaders will only bring those things to the conference that need the church approval or things that the church needs to be informed about.

XX. THE PASTOR AND HIS HEALTH

The pastor should strive to take care of his body because it's the only one he will have in this present life. As pastor, you owe it to your family to live as long as possible. If you die an early death because of the lack of discipline in your eating and a lack of exercising, first of all, you cheat your wife, children and grandchildren of days, months and years they could have had with you.

And you cheat the church of the many sermons that are so beneficial to their spiritual growth. You force the church to go through the pain of looking for and electing a new pastor all because you were too selfish to discipline yourself to take care of your body. I read somewhere where it said, for every hour of exercise, it increases your life expectancy by two hours. You should want to give your family and your church that extra time with you.

XXI. <u>THE PASTOR'S SPIRITUAL LIFE</u>

The pastor spiritual connection is what pastoring is all about and that is what makes you a pastor. Without that connection you are just another man. It's important that you retain that connection with God by developing a time of daily prayer and staying in the word of God.

Remember learning is an unending process. The more you know about prayer and how to pray, the more you can teach the people of God about when and how to pray. You cannot teach what you don't know about prayer and don't practice.

Jesus taught about prayer and practiced prayer in his life and so should you. Someone said if you are too busy to practice prayer, you are too busy period. So remember, preaching and pastoring is three folds physical, mental and spiritual. It takes all three for you to be your very best for God and his people in pastoring and preaching.

XXII. THE PASTOR DEALING WITH TEMPTATIONS

This is an area where all pastors should take special care and never think you are exempt from. When the tempter comes to you, he will not temp you with temptations off the rack as with buying a suit off the rack in a men store, but your temptations will be tailored just for you. It will fit you like a tailored made suit of clothes.

If sex is your weakness, then YOUR temptation will look, walk, talk and smell just like what you have dreamed about. If eating too much is your weakness, then the cakes, pies and chicken will always be there for you.

That's why *prayer* has to be an integral part of you daily life. You will always be tempted with whatever is your greatest weakness whatever that maybe. Another pastor's weakness may not be yours, but you have a weakness and Satan knows exactly what it is and so do you.

There are some things you should flee from because you can't beat it. There is a story about three young rats in a basement trying to steal the cheese from a rat trap. The conversation went something like this. One young rat said to the other two rats. You two hold down the trap down while I run by the trap real fast and get the cheese. But by that time, an old rat came out of the shadows hopping on three legs and said I tried that and it didn't work. The best thing you three can do is to leave that trap along, because it is made to catch rats.

When a pastor knows his weakness, he should leave that along and flee from it because he can't beat it. Temptations will be with you as long as you live. I am told that as long a dog is alive, he will be pestered with fleas. But as soon as the dog dies, every flea will leave him. So it is with pastors and temptations.

Hold High the Torch

Hold the high the torch!
You did not light its glow—
Twas given you by other hands, you know,
Tis yours to keep it burning bright,
Yours to pass on when you no more need light;
For there are other feet that we must guide,
And other forms go marching by our side;
Their eyes are watching every smile and tear
An effort, which we think, are not worthwhile,
Are sometimes just the very help they need,
Actions to which their souls would give most heed.

Author Unknown

Made in United States
Orlando, FL
03 October 2025